Passive Houses

energy efficient homes

The Deutsche Nationalbibliothek lists this publication in the Deutsche Nationalbibliografie; detailed bibliographical data are available on the internet at http://dnb.d-nb.de.

ISBN 978-3-03768-106-0
© 2012 by Braun Publishing AG
www.braun-publishing.ch

1st edition 2012

Editor: Chris van Uffelen
Editorial staff: Lisa Rogers
Graphic concept: Manuela Roth, Berlin
Layout: Theresa Beckenbauer

All of the information in this volume has been compiled to the best of the editor's knowledge. It is based on the information provided to the publisher by the architects' and designers' offices and excludes any liability. The publisher assumes no responsibility for its accuracy or completeness as well as copyright discrepancies and refers to the specified sources (architects' and designers' offices). All rights to the photographs are property of the photographer (please refer to the picture credits).

Chris van Uffelen

Passive Houses

energy efficient homes

BRAUN

Content

Right: Carl Spitzweg: The poor poet, 1839. Oil on canvas, 36.2 x 44.6 cm, Neue Pinakothek, Munich.

Preface

Since the 1970s, energy-saving and ecological techniques have come to affect all aspects of life; even becoming an integral part of politics. The first regulated and standardized low-energy houses appeared first in Sweden and then in Denmark. Since 1991, the Passive House has been setting new standards for architecture, especially in terms of single-family homes. The first standardized Passive House, designed by Wolfgang Feist and built by the architects Bott, Ridder and Westermeier, comprised four semi-detached houses in Darmstadt-Kranichstein. It was in 1988 that Feist, together with Swedish professor Bo Adamson, first defined what a Passive House should entail. He later founded the German Passivhaus Institut in Darmstadt in 1996; today, this institution still sets the standards for Passive House certification. Between 1999 and 2001, the CEPHEUS program (Cost Efficient Passive Houses as European Standards) was responsible for the construction of 221 residential units across in five European countries, increasing the total number of Passive Houses threefold. Oehler Faigle Archkom built the first standalone Passive House family home in Bretten in 1998, one year before the less rigorous low-energy standard regulation was introduced in Germany. Low-energy housing standards demands an annual heating requirement of less than 70kWh per square meter, whereas a Passive House requires less than 15 kWh/(m²a) – this minimal heating demand (or cooling in warm regions) makes conventional central heating (or air conditioning) unnecessary. The conventional "active" systems get replaced by "passive" systems, systems that function due to the organization of building parts and systems, these do not use external primary energy but are operated by the house itself.

The definition of Passive House permits 15kWh/(m²a) maximum heating or alternativly a peak heat load of 10 W/m². Further demands of the Passive House standard are that the building envelope has an air tightness of $n50 \leq 0,6$/hour (blower door test) and that the primary energy demand is below a 120kWh/(m²a) limit including all electrical appliances (heating/cooling, water and electricity). It is plain to see that Passive Houses around the world use different techniques to meet these requirements. While a house above 60° latitude would need a 335 milimeter thick insulation to stay below the required 10 W/m² peak load, a house in Australia needs intensive cooling, this can be achieved by gathering rainwater, for example. In Thailand, a Passive House needs Energy Recovery Ventilation to reduce the humidity load and meet the last demand, which requires that all the demands are met with no loss of comfort.

The open definition of a Passive House neither confines it to one particular building type – Passive House offices have become popular recently, as have kindergartens and factories – nor to one particular material – wood can be used, as can concrete or even snythetics. Passive Houses are environmentally-friendly because of their energy-saving properties, meaning that they do not necessarily need to be ecological in other aspects as well, they also do not have to be sustainable or 'green' (e.g. in terms of ecological footprint, life cycle assessment). The embodied energy involved in constructing a temporary summer pavilion from local recycled materials naturally makes it a much 'greener' option than building a highly-insulated shelter for one season. However, in terms of more usual and durable buildings, the Passive House is one of the most advanced sustainable building options. The extra cost of passive building pays off within a few years and, of course, the more expensive energy prices become, the faster the extra building expense is paid off. Furthermore, passive buildings guarantee quiet, constant ambient conditions, which makes working and living in them more comfortable: opening a window just has a very temporary effect on temperature and humidity, which quickly stabilize after windows are closed. Finally, most Passive Houses are ecological in more than just the passive aspect. Being aware of the advantages of this kind of building often goes hand-in-hand with awareness of other aspects of 'green' design (graywater, recycling and low-pollution materials) and intensive solar harvesting by efficient new solar modules. Combining this awareness with Passive House regulations can then result in a Zero- or even Plus-Energy House.

Different techniques can be used to build a Passive House; some of these are suitable for all climates, others just for specific regions. To meet the four demands listed above, the houses usually employ are range of techniques, although with different prioritization. The most important factor is the use of Superinsulation, which reduces heat transfer to a minimum (high R-values like Rip40 for walls and Rip60 for the roof and low U-values from 0.10 to 0.15 W/(m²/K) are typical). This accompanies an Airtight Construction with air barriers that control air leakage into and out of the building and the careful air sealing of construction joints. Airtightness demands Controlled Ventilation: a mechanical heat recovery ventilation system that constantly provides fresh air is typical for a Passive House. Sometimes the intake air for the ventilation system is pre-heated or pre-cooled by earth warming tubes in the soil (earth-to-air exchangers). The ventilation system incorporates fresh air temperature control as the only kind of heating/cooling system, no radiators or air conditioners are installed. Different heating and cooling elements and a mechanical dehumidifying system can be part of the air supply system. Usually, Space Heating by waste heat from lighting, household appliances and other electrical devices should suffice. In addition to Superinsulation, the building envelope often features Advanced Window Technology: triple-pane, double-low-e insulated glazing, air-seals and specially developed thermally broken window frames result in high R-values and low U-values (from 0.85 to 0.70 W/(m²K) for window pane plus frame). Optimized Daylighting (windows, skylights light tubes, reflective surfaces) reduces the primary energy consumption and provides comfort. When additional light is needed, the use of energy-saving lighting techniques, like light-emitting diode-lamps is preferred. Windows used in Passive Solar Design are oriented towards the equator to make use of direct sunlight, while on the other building side the envelope is as kept as closed as possible. In Central Europe, the northern façade faces the colder conditions, while the south often features large, glazed façades that gain heat even in mid-winter. To prevent overheating in summer peaks, cantilevered roofs provide shade when the sun is high. In warm regions, Passive Solar Design uses brise soleils to reduce the heat. However, Passive Solar Design goes further than direct sun-use and shielding: walls and floors are used to collect, store, and distribute the solar energy all over the house (internal thermal mass). A massive heat storage can collect heat in summer and disperse it in winter (or the other way round). Another aspect of Passive Solar Design is the compact shape of the buildings. This reduces the surface size, so that the area to be insulated is smaller. Especially in warm regions, Energy-Efficient Landscaping is another important technique: trees and pergolas outside the building provide shade and vertical gardens on the walls and greened roofs are a natural source of insulation, absorbing solar energy. The positioning on the plot of land is also an important factor to be taken into consideration.

However, differences do not just exist between the climatic zones, even Germany, Austria and Switzerland have their own requirement specification for Passive Houses; despite the first two being members of the European Union. So being a Passive House or not can differ by a few kilometers (politically and climatically). The certification by the Darmstadt Passivhaus Institut (this has recently broken ties with the only Passive House certifier in the USA) is voluntary, so there is no final indication of what a Passive House should be like, despite the fact that energy use is measurable.

Inuit village Oopungnewing near Frobisher Bay on Baffin Island based on sketches by Charles Francis Hall, mid-19th century.

Eyelid House South Yarra

Melbourne, Australia
Architect: Fiona Winzar Architects
Completion: 2007
Client: Joanne Higginson and Shaun Smith
Certificates and standards: Australian 5 Star Energy Rating
Sustainable techniques: Solar hot water, high insulation, passive heating/cooling, thermal mass, water storage, renewable timber framing and lining
Photos: Emma Cross, Melbourne

Turning this tight and difficult inner city site into a home for a family of five is an important contribution to contemporary and sustainable design practice, where issues of energy efficiency and waste loom large in society. The rear addition to this Victorian terraced house features a roof form that has been manipulated like an eyelid to prevent any overlooking from the neighboring three-story giant and to provide shade and weather protection to the rear glass façade. Energy usage is primarily reduced by passive design features. An arabesque interior, including modern stained glass and routed ply screens, creates an exotic ambiance that complements the owners' collection of old Turkish rugs and furniture.

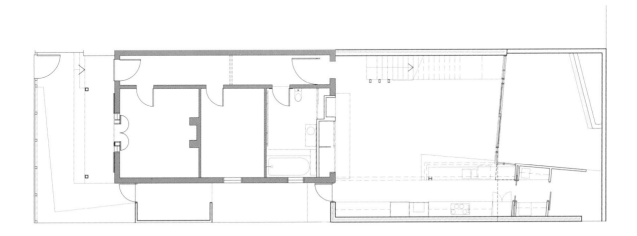

Left: Roof form offers privacy from neighboring apartments.
Right: Ground floor plan.

Top: Private and compact residential space for a family living in the city.
Bottom: Natural materials give warmth to the open plan living area.
Right: Upper level bedroom features a tessellated ply ceiling.

Libeskind Villa

Datteln, Germany
Architect: Studio Daniel Libeskind
Completion: 2009
Client: proportion GmbH
Certificates and standards: KfW40
Sustainable techniques: Solar thermal system, thermal insulation, photovoltaic modules, geothermal heat pump system
Photos: Frank Marburger

The Libeskind Villa is a dynamic signature series home that can be constructed anywhere in the world. Like a crystal growing from rock, the Villa creates a new dialogue between contemporary living and a completely new experience of space. Built from premium wood and zinc, this German-made, sculptural living space meets the highest standards of design, craftsmanship and sustainability. In addition to the design standards, it complies with some of the toughest energy-saving standards worldwide. The villa awakens the senses: light floods through glass expanses, clean lines invite calm while elegant halls and staircases offer seamless transitions.

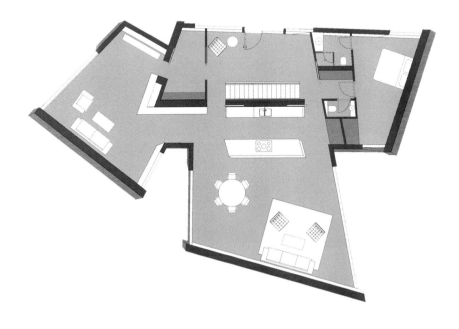

Left: Exterior view with terrace.
Right: Ground floor plan.

Top: Front view with entrance.
Bottom: Rear view with detail of the zinc façade.
Right: Interior view of Villa Libeskind.

Geometric Wisconsin House

Two Rivers, WI, USA
Architect: Shane Black Design
Completion: 2008
Client: Confidential
Sustainable techniques: Solar panels
Photos: Deen Wanek, Waterford

The Geometric Wisconsin House, designed and built by Shane Black, is on a rural, wooded lot. It is wood frame construction with Exterior and Insulation Finishing System stucco exterior and parapet roof. There are seven hydronic solar panels mounted 23 meters away from the house that heat a sand bed beneath the first floor and preheat water. The living space is well-insulated and has a continuous vapor barrier to prevent air filtration. The foyer/kitchen area includes color-changing tiles, a stainless steel staircase with illuminated glass steps, illuminated bar top and a bridge crossing the space beneath the almost seven-meter-high ceiling. The master suite has built-in cabinets, black resin floor, walk in shower and toilet hidden behind emerald acrylic panels, as well as handmade illuminated resin sinks, designed by Shane Black.

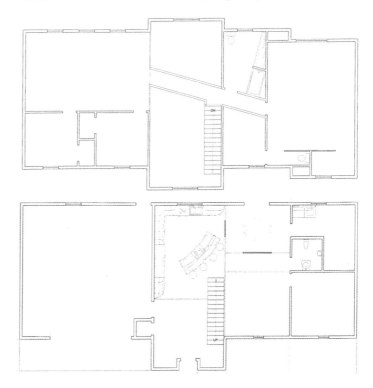

Left: Detail of the illuminated stairs.
Right: Ground floor and first floor plan.

Top: View of northwest.
Bottom: Interior view with kitchen and bar.
Right: View of loft across bridge, stainless steel railing and cable.

Ty Pren Residence

Trallong, United Kingdom
Architect: Feilden Fowles
Completion: 2009
Client: Confidential
Sustainable techniques: Passive heating and cooling, solar collectors, insulation, mechanical ventilation heat recovery system, log boiler, sliding solar shutters, biodigester, accumulator tank, under floor heating
Photos: David Grandorge, London

Ty Pren is a passive long house, inspired by the rich local vernacular of the Brecon Beacons. The passive solar form opens to the south and views towards Pen Y Fan, while the more robust slate cladding protects against the harsh weather from the north. The larch cladding for the solar façades was felled from the client's land two miles away and milled on site. Sixteen larch trees have been planted locally to replace the cladding after twenty-five years, at which time the removed cladding will be burnt to heat the house. A double height central void provides a natural stack for hot air from the stove and solar gains to distribute to the upper floors.

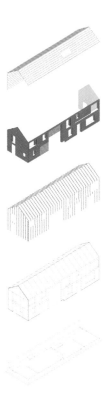

Left: The solar larch façades have deep set reveals in order to increase solar shading.
Right: Constructional build up from slab to cladding.

Top: The form is based on the vernacular Welsh long house typology.
Bottom: The flush detailing of the larch and slate protects the exposed end grain and emphasises the mass of the building.
Right: The building's simple form is expressed as a crisp extrusion.

Red Box

Los Angeles, CA, USA
Architect: Jeremy Levine Design
Completion: 2012
Client: Confidential
Certificates and standards: 2010 California Green Building Standards Code
Sustainable techniques: Thermal chimney for passive cooling, mobile sun shade panels, passive daylighting using interior clerestory windows, drought tolerant landscaping
Photos: Steve Rice, Los Angeles

An unusual feature of this house is the red box that sits on top of a steel frame and acts like an observatory. The box is balanced on a steel frame, which supports the sunscreens that shade the first floor decks, limiting solar heat gain. Interior clerestory windows allow interior rooms to borrow light from each other, dramatically reducing the need for artificial light. All energy needs are met by a photovoltaic array on the roof. Other energy-saving features include mobile sun shade panels that protect the south side of the house from overheating and a thermal chimney that doubles as courtyard space and has bamboo growing out of it. The house cantilevers out over the hill to avoid disturbing the hillside and a limited amount of concrete foundations and retaining walls have been used.

Left: Mobile sun shade panels slide across the South face of the house.
Right: Elevation.

Top: View from west by night.
Bottom: Interior view with glass front and sun shades.
Right: The red box is an observatory which looks across Los Angeles.

The Ellis Residence

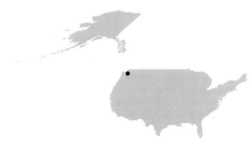

Bainbridge Island, WA, USA
Architect: Coates Design Architects
Completion: 2009
Client: Joanne and Ed Ellis
Certificates and standards: LEED Platinum
Sustainable techniques: Earth-friendly materials, lumber framing, FSC certified rain screen siding, photovoltaic systems, soy based stain and sealant, hybrid insulation system, triple glazed windows
Photos: Roger Turk - Northlight Photography

The Ellis Residence is an example of modern residential design incorporating local environmental concerns, state-of-the-art energy efficiency and visionary educational opportunities for the public. The project embodies the client's vision of home that raises the bar for energy-producing housing while maintaining aesthetics and livability. This LEED Platinum certified home is a milestone in the efforts to create truly sustainable designs. Perched high upon Yeomalt Bluff, this home enjoys a commanding 180-degree view of the Puget Sound and City of Seattle. It features a 70 percent energy use reduction compared to an average North American home through the use of geothermal heat, photovoltaic energy collection, solar hot water and thermal massing.

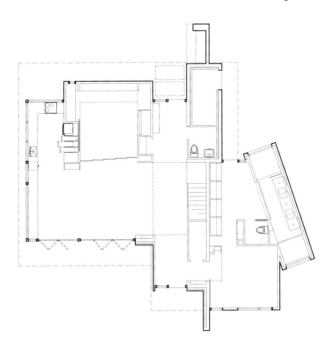

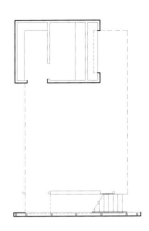

Left: Entrance to the building.
Right: Ground floor and ground floor carport plans.

Top: Exterior view by twilight.
Bottom: Entrance with detail of the façade.
Right: Living room.

(X) villa

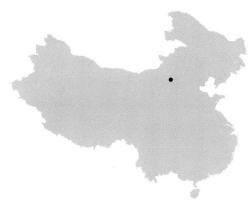

Ordos, China
Architect: *Multiplicities
Completion: 2013
Client: Confidential
Certificates and standards: LEED
Sustainable techniques: Insulation, passive heating and cooling, water storage
Photos: *Multiplicities/Daniel Holguin

The black skin of the (X) villa absorbs heat and provides protection and warmth, creating different programmatic thicknesses and buffer zones wherever necessary. Entering the villa through one of the "X's" funnels, residents and visitors encounter the void that works as an atrium throughout the house. The first patio is the main access to the small living room that overlooks both voids. The second patio is directly linked to the pool and the sauna. The house makes use of passive heating and cooling systems to retain a constantly comfortable temperature. The house is also well insulated, reducing the amount of extra heating needed during the winter months.

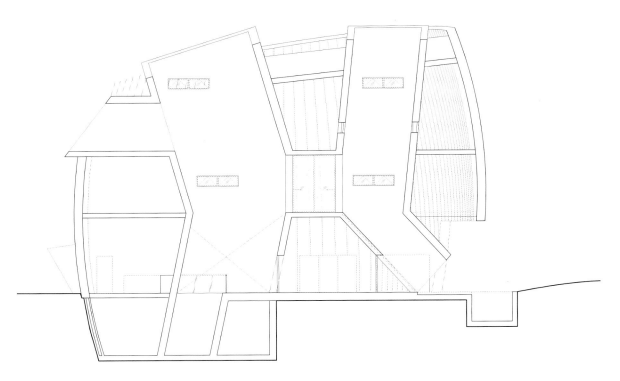

Left: Exterior view with garage.
Right: Section.

Top: Exterior view in landscape.
Bottom: Interior view of corridor.
Right: View to the patio.

Enngisteinstrasse Residence

Worb, Switzerland
Architect: Halle 58 Architekten
Completion: 2011
Client: Confidential
Certificates and standards: Minergie-P
Sustainable techniques: Passive use of solar energy, solar panels heat pump with borehole heat exchanger (heating and water), comfort ventilation with earth-tube collector
Photos: Christine Blaser, Berne

This multi-family house contains three apartments and is situated within the historic center of Worb. The apartments have flexible floor plans, organized around a massive core. The kitchen, dining and living areas create a continuous, flowing space. The apartments are characterized by bright, mixed-use spaces, while the generously proportioned balconies provide a high-quality continuity of the interior space. The new construction is distinguished by its consistent, energy efficiency and ecological construction. A two-story timber construction has been erected on top of the recycled-concrete base and a fir-wood formwork characterizes the façade. The Minergie-P standard was achieved through the passive and active utilization of solar energy and a well-insulated building envelope.

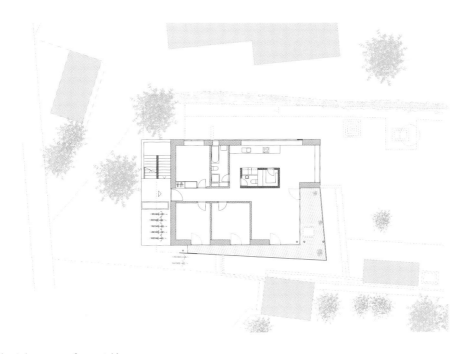

Left: Detail of the staircase, seen from outside.
Right: Site and ground floor plan.

Top: Living and dining area with access to balcony.
Bottom: Balcony with glass façade.
Right: Exterior view with garden.

Danish Smart House Eco

Herfølge, Denmark
Architect: Valbæk Brørup Arkitekter
Completion: 2007
Client: Confidential
Certificates and standards: Nordic Ecolabelling
Sustainable techniques: Solar panels, passive heating/cooling, ventilation with passive heat recovery, insulation
Photos: Anders Beier (44, 46 a.), Mikkel Strange (46 b., 47)

Even at a distance this house is easily visible with its white ceramic façade and slim building volume. The design has clear roots in modern Nordic architecture, with emphasis on daylight, functionality, materials, detailing and contextualization. The house is certified with the Nordic Ecolabelling, which secures the dwellers a healthy environment and indoor climate, together with a low use of energy. The sustainable design optimizes the use of passive sunlight, solar panels, a maximum of insulation due to the thin façade material and an airtight house with a ventilation system with passive heat recovery. The housing system is flexible with regards to building orientation, number of floors, number of rooms and material use.

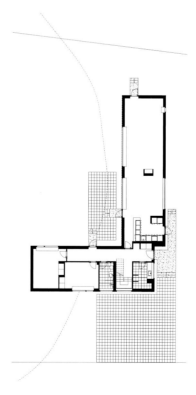

Left: View of the house from the garden.
Right: Ground floor plan.

Top: East façade with white ceramic tiles contrasts warm mahogany windows.
Bottom: Kitchen, showing one of many accesses to the garden.
Right: Open floor plan with living and dining room separated by the fireplace.

Hof

Hofsós, Iceland
Architect: Studio Granda
Completion: 2007
Client: Confidential
Certificates and standards: All Icelandic codes
Sustainable techniques: High insulation, sensible glazing, heavy core
Photos: Sigurgeir Sigurjonsson, Reykjavík

Hof is a country residence situated less than 100 kilometers from the Arctic Circle. The house rises from the tufted site as a series of sheer cedar and concrete walls that will weather according to the vagaries of the elements. The displaced grass of the field has been reinstated on the roof and the surrounding meadow is cut and folded in earthworks of turf and stone. The house is highly insulated and thermally stable due to the massive concrete walls, stone floors and balanced fenestration. Geothermal energy is used for the floor heating and radiators as well as for all domestic use. Electricity use is minimized by design and the little that is required is sourced from hydroelectric and geothermal sources.

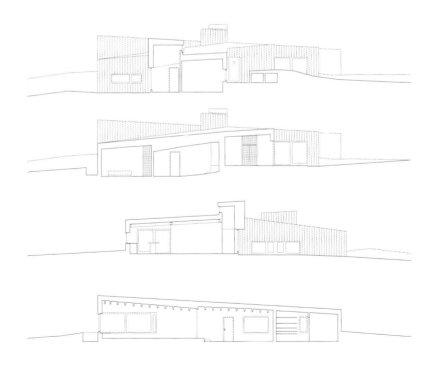

Left: Detail of the living room window.
Right: Section.

Top: Exterior view from southwest.
Bottom: Detail of the cladding.
Right: Dining and kitchen area.

Villa Langenkamp

Ebeltoft, Denmark
Architect: Langenkamp.dk architects
Completion: 2008
Client: Olav Langenkamp & Lotte Dahl
Certificates and standards: Passive House certified
Sustainable techniques: Passive cooling, solar panels, heat pump, geothermal heat
Photos: Thomas Søndergaard, Aarhus

Villa Langenkamp in Ebeltoft is the first certified Passive House in Denmark. This simple and highly modern wooden house has been built from prefabricated Passive House elements. The house displays a compact geometry and clean lines that fit in beautifully with the surrounding landscape, which is full of contrasts with tall, majestic pines and low horizons. The architectural design and the reduced energy consumption both speak of a minimalistic house adapted to the new minimal energy requirements.

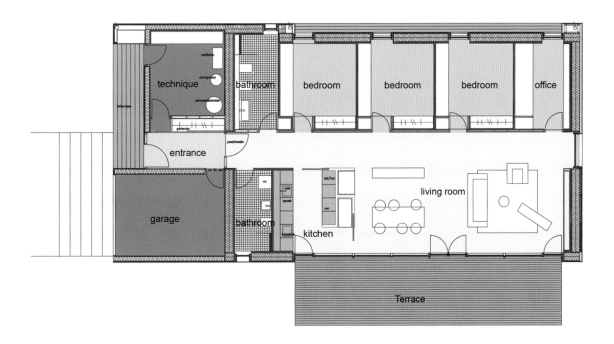

Left: Detail of the façade and entrance.
Right: Ground floor plan.

Top: Northwest façade with terrace.
Bottom: Southwest façade with glass front.
Right: Interior view, kitchen and dining room.

Bersch Passive House

Waldstetten, Germany
Architect: Karl Miller
Completion: 2010
Client: Anja and Benno Bersch
Certificates and standards: Passive House certified, KfW Efficiency House 55
Sustainable techniques: Wood pellet heating, solar collectors for hot water and heating support, heat recovery ventilation with heat exchanger, wood-aluminum windows with three way thermal insulation glazing, insulation cellulose
Photos: Courtesy of the architects

This simple, cubic-shaped house faces the south and will be fitted with a solar power system in the future. The floor plan is organized with living areas facing south and bedrooms facing north. An open stairway leads from the living room to the gallery above. Privacy in the outdoor areas is achieved by an outdoor courtyard located on the property's south border. This area is protected from the street by a wooden wall and the garage. Access to the street from the courtyard is provided by sliding doors. The house is highly insulated with cellulose insulation and renewable, low-energy building materials were used in the construction.

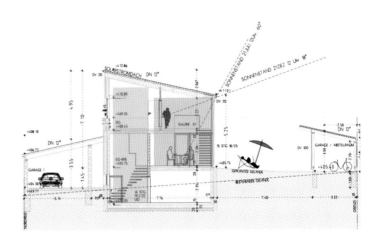

Left: View from garden.
Right: Section.

Top: Street view with entrance.
Bottom: View from south with porch.
Right: Exterior view with garden and terrace.

Maison Passive, 95

Bessancourt, France
Architect: Karawitz Architecture
Completion: 2009
Client: Confidential
Certificates and standards: Passive House certified
Sustainable techniques: Natural materials, extremely low-energy consumption, photovoltaic panels
Photos: Herve Abbadie, Bessancourt

This house has a membrane of bamboo poles, which breaks up the light and creates a unique atmosphere inside. A very important element in the planning is the 'spine'. It consists of 60-centimeter-wide wooden discs and divides the floor plan into two parts. The larger of the two parts part is situated on the southern side and contains the living and sleeping areas, the smaller part is on the northern side and accommodates the sanitary and service/utility rooms. The house was implemented using mainly natural materials – wood panels for the construction, cellulose and wood-fiber for the insulation, plasterboards, biopaints for the interior finishing. The photovoltaic panels on the roof make this house an energy-plus-house, according to the French standard.

Left: Front view with open blinds and solar panels on the roof.
Right: Section.

Top: View from garden with closed blindes.
Bottom: Interior view.
Right: Entry with sink and staircase.

Three Trees

Los Angeles, CA, USA
Architect: Jeremy Levine Design
Completion: 2011
Client: Confidential
Certificates and standards: 2010 California Green Building Standards Code
Sustainable techniques: Rain water collection system, graywater recycling system, grid-tied net-metered solar panels, thermal chimney for passive cooling, thermal rock wall for passive climate control, mobil sun shade panels
Photos: Neil Toussaint

A house built around three trees; this design plays on the idea of a Regional Modernism by merging two of the local architectural styles of the region: the language of thick walls and carved mass of the Spanish Colonial tradition and the modern abstraction and open space of the case study tradition. The existing house was a 'fixer' on a lot filled with big trees. Those same trees boxed in the house, preventing an addition to the home. The solution was to build the addition around the trees, enclosing them into small open courtyards. Every room in the house opens out into a outdoor space with a sheltering tree.

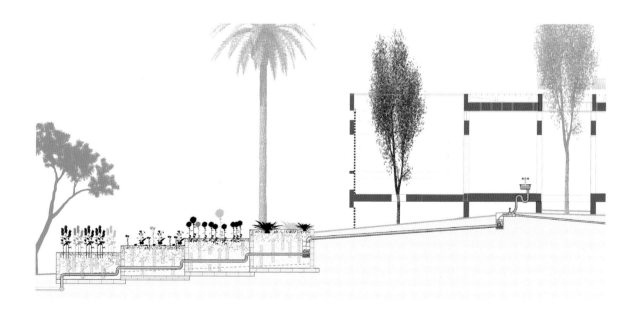

Left: Exterior view from west.
Right: Plan for graywater recycling.

Top: Exterior view from east with driveway.
Bottom: The outdoor room.
Right: Interior view of kitchen.

Palmwood House

London, United Kingdom
Architect: Undercurrent architects
Completion: 2008
Client: Confidential
Sustainable techniques: Brownfield regeneration, use of reused materials, low ecological footprint
Photos: Undercurrent architects

Palmwood House is a prototype building for problematic urban sites; a small, triangular infill lot severely constrained by height restrictions, acute boundaries, failed development plans and conservation controls. The floor plan is split into three areas on the ground floor: an open living/kitchen/dining area, a bedroom and a walled courtyard. Above is another bedroom and a roof terrace that overlooks the courtyard. The design utilizes unique material applications as well as sustainable practices such as brownfield regeneration, low-energy, reused materials and advanced building systems, allowing the building's ecological footprint to reflect its small physical one.

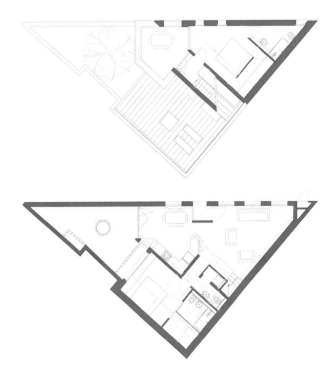

Left: Front view.
Right: Ground and first floor plans.

69

Top: Interior view with staircase.
Bottom: Bedroom with view to garden.
Right: Inner courtyard with balcony.

Tree House

Wilmington, DE, USA
Architect: Sander Architects
Completion: 2006
Client: Confidential
Certificates and standards: LEED Silver
Sustainable techniques: Natural heating/cooling, natural ventilation, daylighting, radiant heat
Photos: Sharon Risedorph Photography, San Francisco

Tree House sits in a residential subdivision surrounded by century-old trees and a seasonal stream. The vertical form allows the house to sit in the trees, and to have marvelous views of the canopy from the two upper floors. Horizontal windows provide select views into the landscape, and a large window in the living room offers dramatic views into the deep woods. The exterior entrance stair, cantilevered away from the façade, enters through a trio of trees and provides a view of the stream as one rises to enter the house. The house uses Energy Star appliances, which have a low-energy consuption, as well as sustainable building materials, such as local stone for the fireplace, recycled aluminum for the staircase, non-toxic paint and low-flow faucets and toilets to conserve water.

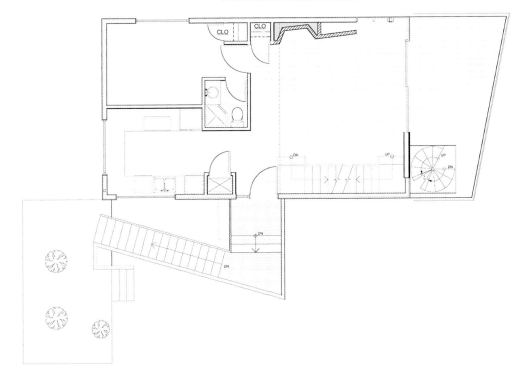

Left: View of the east façade and entry staircase.
Right: Ground floor plan.

Top: The house glows at dusk.
Bottom: Living room with view through the ancient woods.
Right: Entry stairs showing aluminum bar grate designed to shed snow.

HA08

Ottenbach, Germany
Architect: Patrick Schiller Architektur
Completion: 2010
Client: Confidential
Certificates and standards: KFW-Effizienzhaus 70
Sustainable techniques: Thermal insulation composite system, triple glazing
Photos: Courtesy of the architects

This affordable family house has been designed to accommodate a family with two children and is located on the edge of a nature conservation area, near the river Krumm, with a view of the surrounding greenery. The building is divided into two parts; one is flat-roofed and contains the garage and storage rooms, while the other has an asymmetrical saddle roof and houses the residential space. The house has a compact and well-insulated envelope with a glazed ground floor, optimizing solar gain. The house is heated by a warm air pump and the window openings have been positioned to allow natural cooling and rapid ventilation.

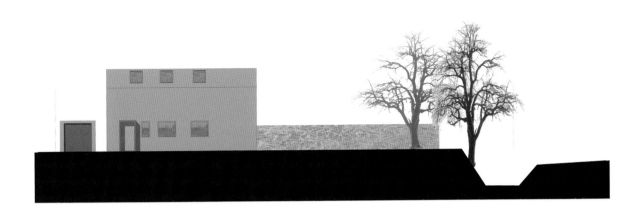

Left: Street view with entrance.
Right: Elevation.

Top: View from south with garage.
Bottom: Exterior view.
Right: East view with terrace.

Villa Nyberg

Borlänge, Sweden
Architect: Kjellgren Kaminsky Architecture
Completion: 2010
Client: Nyberg family
Certificates and standards: Swedish Passive House standards
Sustainable techniques: Solar panels, passive heating, wooden façade, well insulated windows, doors, walls, floors and roof
Photos: Kalle Sanner

In 2009 Kjellgren Kaminsky Architecture produced Sweden's first series of passive type houses. The architect's goal is to make this environmentally friendly building technique available for all. Villa Nyberg is a customized house, built for the Nyberg family in Borlänge, central Sweden. The living room and kitchen open up towards the views of the lake, while the more private areas such as the bedrooms and bathrooms are situated on the other side of the house with smaller windows overlooking the forest. The round shape of the villa eliminates cold-bridges and reduces the enclosing wall area of the house. The round shape also effects the way the residents live in the house, moving from room to room around the building experiencing different views and daylight conditions.

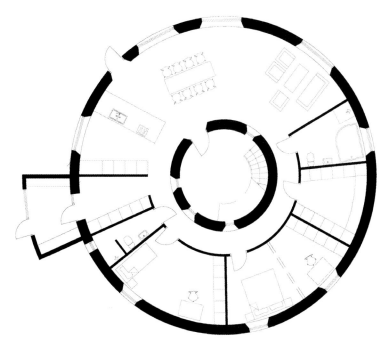

Left: Exterior view from lake side.
Right: Ground floor plan.

Top: Interior view towards lake.
Bottom: Living room.
Right: Northern façade with smaller windows.

Konkol Residence

Hudson, WI, USA
Architect: TE Studio
Completion: 2010
Client: Gary Konkol
Certificates and standards: Passive House certified, MN GreenStar Gold
Sustainable techniques: Earth-friendly materials and construction, solar panels, passive solar, geothermal
Photos: Chad Holder, Minneapolis

This Passive House is a three-bedroom, two-story single family home with walk-out basement level, and a rooftop terrace. This home is the first certified Passive House in the state of Wisconsin. It sits on a 4,047-square-meter plot in the town of Hudson, Wisconsin – just a few minutes from interstate 94. Located on the outer edge of a residential development, the home overlooks the St. Croix river valley. The building lot provides stunning views and prime passive solar exposure. With its renewable energy systems, it is projected to make more energy than it consumes and be carbon neutral for operation.

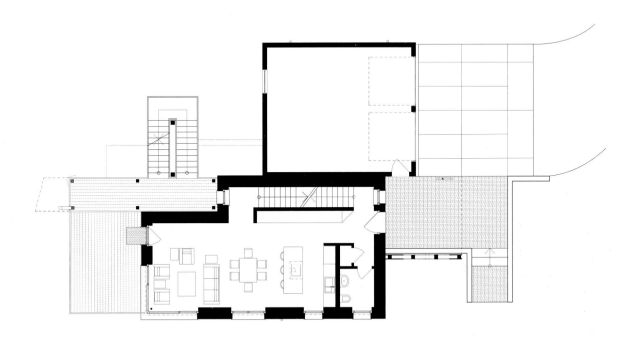

Left: Northeast entry elevation.
Right: Ground floor plan.

Top: Southeast perspective with solar tracker.
Bottom: Second floor deck, reading area.
Right: Exterior stair from lower level to rooftop terrace.

Passive House Kamakura

Kamakura, Japan
Architect: Key Architects
Completion: 2009
Client: Taro Hasumi
Certificates and standards: Passive House certified
Sustainable techniques: High level of insulation, air tight, low-energy consumption
Photos: Courtesy of the architects

Passive House Kamakura was the first certified Passive House to be built in Japan. With the construction of this house, the architects wanted to convince people in Japan that there is no danger in insulating buildings and constructing them so that they are air-tight, if the moisture movement is properly considered. Saving energy during the construction period was also a very important issue for the architects. The main goal of the architects in constructing Passive House in Kamakura was to prove that the high level of insulation and air-tightness would actually contribute to energy-savings. It was recognized that the demand for heating would be rendered virtually unnecessary by installing just 240 millimeters of wood fiber insulation.

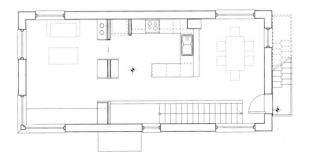

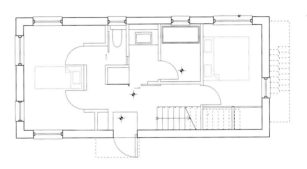

Left: Detail of the charcoaled cedar cladding.
Right: Ground and first floor plans.

Top: Southeast corner with window.
Bottom: East elevation of building.
Right: View of the open plan kitchen.

Minergie Family Home

Zollikon, Switzerland
Architect: Schwarz & Schwarz Architekten
Completion: 2010
Client: Andreas Schwarz
Certificates and standards: Minergie
Sustainable techniques: Highly insulated, heat pumps with geothermal probes, controlled ventilation, free cooling via heat pump in summer
Photos: Bruno Helbling, Zürich and Markus Fischer, Uster

Built in 1920, this family house has been replaced with a terraced house, marking the corner location of Brandis street and Bauis street. The horizontal emphasis of the different levels adapts to the sloping site, while the filler wall, with its twists, asymmetry and vertical orientation gives the impression of movement in the façade. The stories have been twisted in their arrangement, giving them plasticity. An annex was added to the property to improve the view from the upper floors, raising them slightly and thus allowing a better view of the lake. The living room is the central room in the house. The house has been awarded the Minergie Standard certificate.

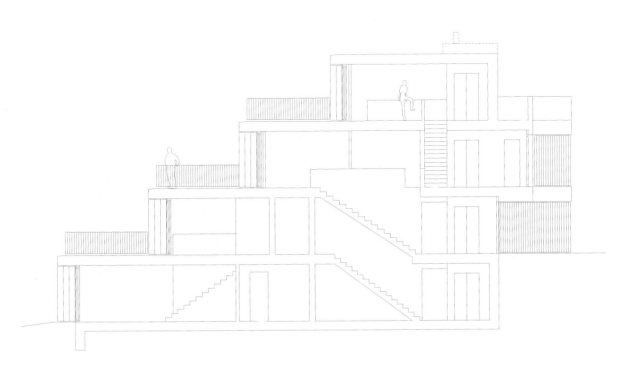

Left: Exterior view by twilight.
Right: Section.

Top: Front view with garden, terrace and balconies.
Bottom: Street view with entrance.
Right: Interior view with entrance and staircase.

House Annen

Farschweiler, Germany
Architect: Architekten Stein Hemmes Wirtz
Completion: 2011
Client: Confidential
Certificates and standards: Plus Energy House, 1st place innovation award RWE heat pump
Sustainable techniques: Photovoltaic/solar thermal plant, CO_2 neutral, natural building materials
Photos: Courtesy of the architects

This Plus Energy house in Farschweiler uses the requirements of the building construction to characterize the design, instead of viewing them as a disadvantage. The house has a saddle roof and has been designed as a family residence, on a plot of land in a newly developed area of Farschweiler, at the edge of the Hochwald. The simple shape of the house arose from energy considerations and takes the form of a closed building envelope, without bay windows or other projecting or retreating features, as this improves insulation. Other important design decisions were also made in favor of sustainability; these were executed with a fine feel for the overall design result.

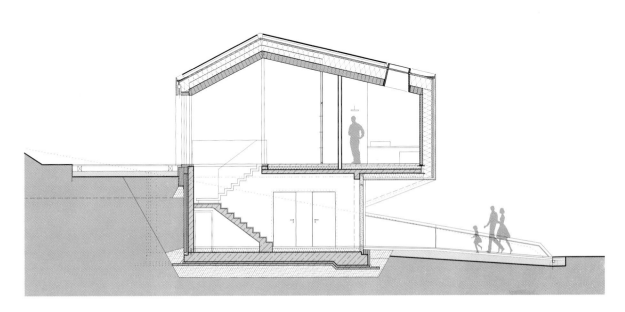

Left: Exterior view with garden.
Right: Section.

Top: Front view and compact volume.
Bottom: Entrance area with detail of façade.
Right: Interior view of bathroom.

Standard House

Pszczyna, Poland
Architect: KWK Promes
Completion: 2010
Client: Confidential
Sustainable techniques: Thermal insulation
Photos: Mariusz Czechowicz-Murator

The main goal for this project was to design a house that fits every plot. The round shape of the house makes it suitable for any given shape of the site, freedom in the choice of a roof type makes it universal in terms of landscape conditionings, while interior flexibility allows it to adopt to the needs of an individual family. Sustainability stands at the focal point of the design: The house was designed to respect the environment by choosing natural building materials and using renewable energy sources. The optimal building shape, very good thermal insulation, elimination of thermal bridges and renewable energy installations all contribute to the sustainable and energy efficient design.

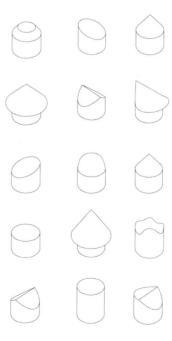

Left: Front view from garden with terrace.
Right: Typological schematics.

Top: *Rear view of the building.*
Bottom: *View by night.*
Right: *Detail of the wooden façade.*

Hi'ilani EcoHouse

Honokaa, HI, USA
Design: Studio RMA
Completion: 2012
Client: Confidential
Certificates and standards: Designed to obtain LEED Platinum
Sustainable techniques: Solar panels, full rain water catchment for drinking water and irrigation, passive cooling, wind turbines, solar pumps
Photos: Robert Mechielsen, Topanga (104, 106 b.), Sarah Anderson, Honokaa (106 a.), Teresa Sugg, Honokaa (107)

The Hi'ilani EcoHouse is a carbon-neutral designed, two-family residence, ready for grid independence. The structure, including the roof, is built with Structural Concrete Insulated Panels (SCIP). These panels have a EPS foam core, a three-dimensional wire truss welded through them with wire meshes at each side. A final coat of concrete creates a structure high in strength and insulation. The Hi'ilani EcoHouse leverages the trade winds to cool the home. It uses a rainwater catchment for drinking water. Several solar systems provide the home with electricity. This high-end home has a spa, recording facility, offices, a full media room and an in-house small hospice, all designed to operate off the local grid.

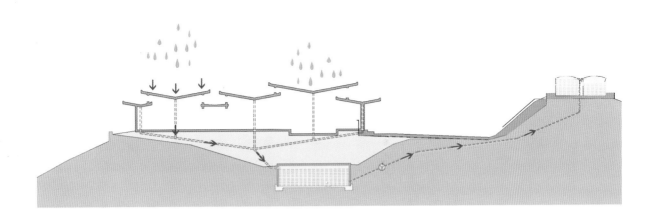

Left: Details of the windows and roof overhangs.
Right: Water catchment plan.

Top: View into the geometry of the main living room prior to windows.
Bottom: Close-up of roof overhang.
Right: View of the Pacific from living room.

Frame House

Invermere, BC, Canada
Architect: The marc boutin architectural collaborative
Completion: 2008
Client: Confidential
Sustainable techniques: Solar panels, geothermal heating/cooling, passive heating/cooling, natural cross ventilation, water storage
Photos: Bruce Edwards (108, 110), Patrick Chenier (111)

This house was conceived of as an object sitting within a recreational landscape. The house is not only the space for living, but also a tool by which one's senses of the natural environment are heightened. The house is an articulated 'frame' containing a public volume and a private core. It integrates sustainable design strategies, including natural ventilation, passive solar gain, a geothermal field, and solar hot water heating. As a result, the house exists virtually off-the-grid, maximizing its poetic value and minimizing its impact upon the site itself. The northwest side of the house is a controlled, opaque façade. The southeast side of the house is an operable glazed façade, which opens to the mountains.

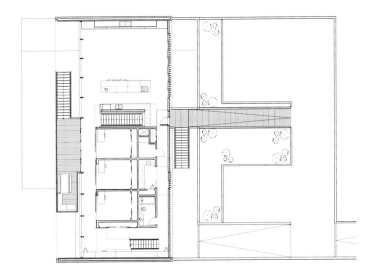

Left: View form southwest with swimming pool.
Right: Ground floor plan.

Top: North elevation with mountains in the background.
Bottom: View from southeast with glass façade.
Right: Panoramic dining room.

Prescott Passive House

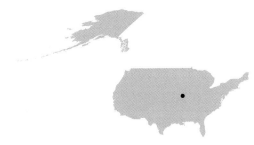

Kansas City, KS, USA
Architect: Studio 804
Completion: 2010
Client: built as spec house
Certificates and standards: Passive House certified and LEED Platinum
Sustainable techniques: Passive heating/cooling, louvers, thermal mass, high performance windows, super insulation, southern orientation,energy recovery ventilator, small footprint
Photos: Courtesy of studio804, photographer: Lawrence

The Prescott Passive House is a single-family, low-energy residence located in Kansas City, Kansas. This unique house is designed for the affordable housing market as a spec house that will sell to qualified buyers, those with an annual income of no more than eighty percent of the target Area Median Income (AMI). Designed to exceed both Passive House and LEED Platinum standards, the residence uses minimal energy through affordable passive means. The home is located in the Prescott neighborhood, which, despite being just minutes from downtown Kansas City, remains a neighborhood in transition not unlike the rest of the derelict urban core that typifies the city.

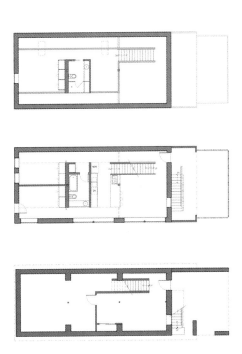

Left: Interior view of the living room, hallway, kitchen and loft space.
Right: Basement, main level and loft level plans.

Top: South façade of Prescott Passive House.
Bottom: Detail of the north façade.
Right: South and east façades of Prescott Passive House.

The Camden Passive House

London, United Kingdom
Architect: Bere:architects
Completion: 2010
Client: Confidential
Certificates and standards: Passive House certified
Sustainable techniques: Passive heating/cooling, insulation, triple glazing, mechanical ventilation with heat recovery, low-energy LED lighting, solar thermal panels, rainwater storage, two green roofs
Photos: Tim Crocker (116, 118), Jefferson Smith (119)

The Camden Passive House is the first certified Passive House in London. The primary objective was to achieve a comfortable home for a young family whilst minimizing energy consumption. The 118-square-meter family house, split over two floors with two wild flower meadow roofs and a south-facing garden, is constructed with a heavily insulated prefabricated timber frame. Designed to use 13kWh/(m²a) for heating, with healthy air and water quality prioritized with non-toxic materials and heat recovery ventilation. Mains water use is supplemented by an underground water-harvesting tank providing water for irrigation. CO_2 emissions are minimized with excellent insulation, draught free construction, triple glazed windows and a solar thermal panel.

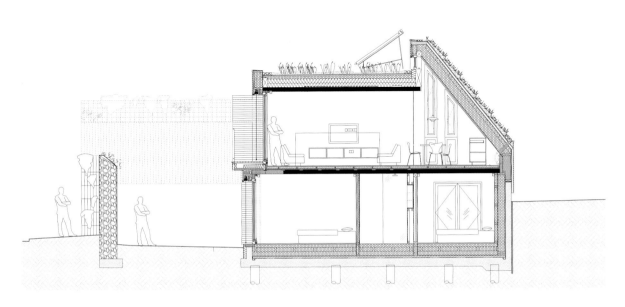

Left: Entrance to the house.
Right: Section.

Top: Front view from south.
Bottom: Interior first floor living room.
Right: Rear courtyard.

Glass Townhouse

Venice, CA, USA
Architect: Sander Architects
Completion: 2010
Client: Confidential
Certificates and standards: LEED Silver
Sustainable techniques: Natural heating/cooling, natural ventilation, daylighting, wired for solar panels
Photos: Sharon Risedorph Photography, San Francisco

This building has been built using recycled construction materials. It is divided vertically down the middle to create a pair of three-story condominiums designed for the client on one side and his parents on the other. Playful architectural details include double-height translucent walls, exposed steel structure, cutouts in interior walls, and plywood railings and ceiling finishes. The exterior skin of the building is a double-layer of translucent materials: multi-cell acrylic panels provide the waterproofing inside lapped scales of glass. Passive heating/cooling are used to maintain a comfortable temperature and the house is super-insulated with blue-jean insulation.

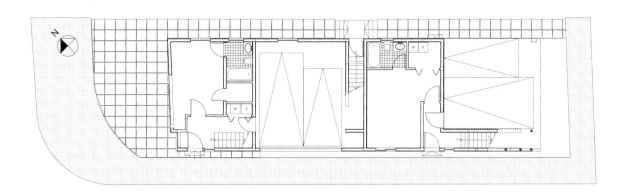

Left: Stairwell, different interior levels.
Right: Ground floor plan.

Top: Exterior view of southern wall of glass.
Bottom: Interior stairs with glass wall and steel railings.
Right: Glass layered over translucent panels on south façade.

The Skinny

Philadelphia, PA, USA
Architect: Interface Studio Architects
Completion: 2010
Client: Postgreen Homes
Certificates and standards: LEED Platinum, Energy Star, HERS 24
Sustainable techniques: Solar hot water, highly insulated building envelope, photovoltaics
Photos: Sam Oberter

The recent housing bubble has driven American houses to extreme sizes and exurban locations. Low-cost mortgages have helped to foster a culture of bigger is better. The Skinny is part of the Skinny Homes project and is a three-unit deployment of the 100K House initiative, providing small, efficient and affordable options for first-time Philadelphia homebuyers. The Skinny Homes have received LEED Platinum ratings and use 76 percent less energy than a typical American home. The houses feature recycled and locally sourced products; they are well insulated and air sealed, utilize downsized and efficient HVAC systems and feature photovoltaic solar panels. The homes utilize double-stud wall construction, allowing them to have thick, super-insulated walls.

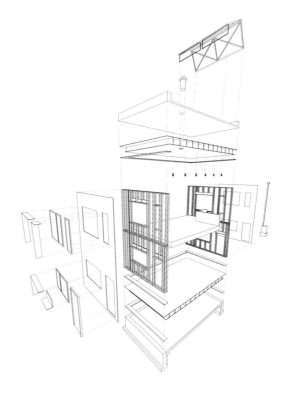

Left: Façade with screen printed cladding.
Right: Component axonometric.

Top: Side façade showing cladding and sunshades.
Bottom: View of open riser stair and kitchen beyond.
Right: Front façade.

Line House

Skummeslövsstrand, Sweden
Architect: Ziphouse /Ejje Lundgren
Completion: 2010
Client: Zip house
Certificates and standards: Swedish Passive House certified
Sustainable techniques: Insulation
Photos: Peter Guthrie (128,130 a., 131), Anna Attola (130 b.)

Ziphouse produces low-cost prefab Passive Houses with modern designs for every day family living. The building system is a refinement of a 'standard' SIP (Structural Insulated Panel). It is 100 percent damp proof, extremely airtight and well insulated, making this house the only one certified according to the Swedish government's strict regulations on passive housing. Combined with highly efficient windows and foundations, the house does not require any active heating even when the temperature drops to -20 degrees Celsius. The architecture is based on an idea of a line which runs up and down, to the left and to the right, inside and outside creating walls, roofs, benches and so on which change both direction and function at each turn.

Left: View of house with integrated carport and entrance.
Right: Ground floor plan.

Top: *Exterior view with terrace.*
Bottom: *Living room.*
Right: *Exterior view.*

Passive House Gerasdorf

Gerasdorf, Austria
Architect: Abendroth Architekten
Completion: 2007
Client: Confidential
Certificates and standards: Passive House certified by PHI Darmstadt, klima:aktiv Passive House
Sustainable techniques: Compact ventilation unit with heat recovery and heating coil, air preheating by ground heat exchanger
Photos: Andreas Buchberger, Vienna

This Passive House is accessed through a light wooden construction that closes the land towards the east and helps provide privacy. The high-rising wooden slats on the sides of the roof terrace provide the family with an airy outdoor space for sunbathing, protected from view. An opening around the corner leads you into the massively walled Passive House cuboid. All necessary circulation in the house runs along the massive back wall on the north side that has a high heat storage capacity. The ground floor offers a generous space for a family life. The clear, compact volume of the house, expands in dimensions towards the south, giving the windows a perfect solar orientation, thus displaying the massive construction.

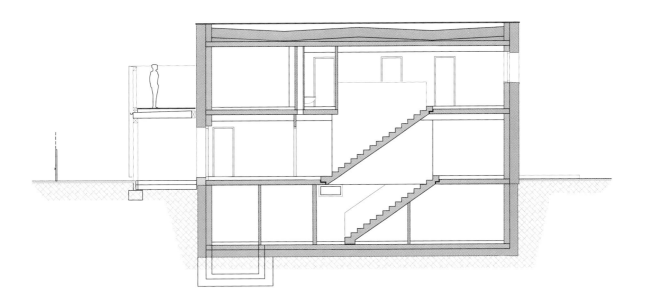

Left: Carport and entrance.
Right: Section.

Top: View from street to carport.
Bottom: View from southwest by twilight.
Right: Sun deck.

Passive House Vogel

Sattel, Switzerland
Architect: Diethelm & Spillmann Architekten
Completion: 2010
Client: Samuel Vogel
Certificates and standards: Minergie-P
Sustainable techniques: Wood elements and solid core, photovoltaic systems, heating/hot water using solar thermal (hot water tank), stove with hot water heat exchanger
Photos: Roger Frei, Zurich

The location of this Passive House offers stunning views of the surrounding mountain landscape and of Lake Aegeri. The living area is raised up on an unheated base, which houses the garage and basement. Because planning restrictions only allowed for a two-story construction, the house stretches along the horizontal plane, resulting in a characteristic overhang. Inside, silver-painted plaster meets the untreated larch wood panels. Externally, the building is wrapped in a dark-varnished wood cladding and the roof is completely covered with photovoltaic and solar thermal elements, giving the building a unified appearance.

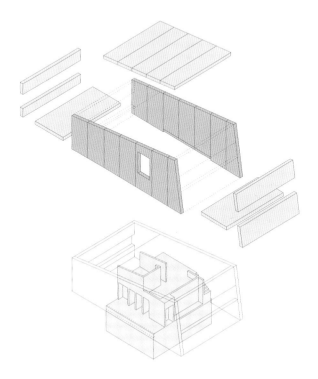

Left: Northeast façade with panoramic window.
Right: Exploded view.

Top: Terrace with staircase.
Bottom: Southeast façade, with a massive base that controls the terrain.
Right: Entrance with built-in wardrobe and doors to the private rooms.

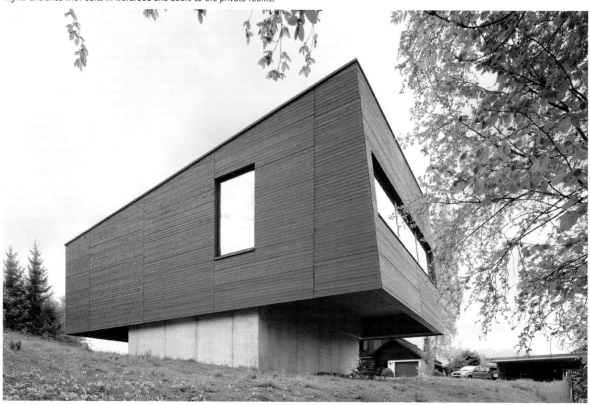

Villa C

Odense, Denmark
Architect: Langenkamp.dk architects
Completion: 2010
Client: Confidential
Certificates and standards: Passive House certified
Sustainable techniques: Geothermal heat, heat pump
Photos: Courtesy of the architects

Villa C is a two-story, single-family house situated in rural surroundings, yet close to the city of Odense in Denmark. The house is formed from two intersecting squares, which illustrate the mixed functionality of the house. Traditional living quarters are combined with a smaller extension, which holds the offices of a private psychology practice. An excellent indoor climate is among other factors achieved by floor heating controlled by a compact unit linked to five vertical helix probes for space heating and to supply domestic hot water. In summertime, the system can be reversed to cool the indoor temperature.

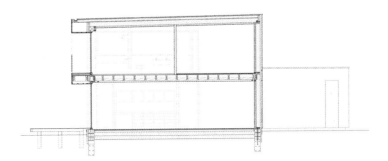

Left: Exterior view with terrace and façade detail.
Right: Section.

Top: Front view of terrace and balcony.
Bottom: View from kitchen to garden.
Right: Detail of the façade and view of rural surroundings.

Leicester House

Asheville, NC, USA
Architect: SPG Architects
Completion: 2009
Client: Confidential
Sustainable techniques: Geothermal field, green roof on lower level, reflective white roof on upper level, rainwater collection
Photos: Daniel Levin

This hilltop residence, located at the edge of a wooded knoll in the rolling foothills of the Blue Ridge Mountains, has expansive southern and western views. Approaching through a dense wood, one arrives at a striking single story façade of Corten steel in a wood frame. Functionality and energy efficiency are achieved both by this programmatic zoning as well as the careful choice of materials, fixtures, fittings and energy. The house uses geothermal energy. The green roof on the lower level helps to insulate the house while a reflective white roof on the upper level helps to prevent overheating. Rainwater is also collected and recycled.

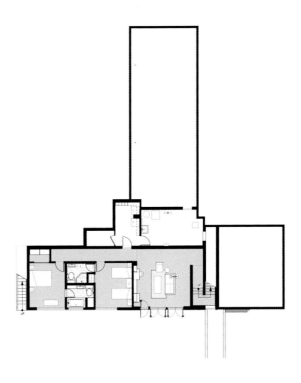

Left: Rear façade.
Right: Ground floor plan.

Top: Front view with lower und upper level.
Bottom: Detail of the Corten steel façade.
Right: Green roof over lower level.

The Larch House

Ebbw Vale, United Kingdom
Architect: Bere:architects
Completion: 2010
Client: United Welsh Housing Association
Certificates and standards: Code Six Zero Carbon Certified Passive House
Sustainable techniques: Passive heating/cooling, insulation, triple glazing, mechanical ventilation with heat recovery, low-energy LED lighting, plus photovoltaic panels and solar thermal panels, rainwater storage
Photos: Jefferson Smith

The Larch House is the United Kingdom's first Code Six Zero Carbon, low cost certified Passive House, built as prototype social housing. The three-bedroom house has been built 30 meters above sea level in an exposed and misty hilltop location. In spite of this, most energy needs are met by heat from the sun, occupants and appliances. The house generates as much energy from the sun in the summer months as it uses for the whole year, making it Zero Carbon , following the United Kingdom's definition, and showing how we can reduce household energy bills and protect people from fuel poverty, helping to ensure that we live comfortably with minimal impact on the natural world.

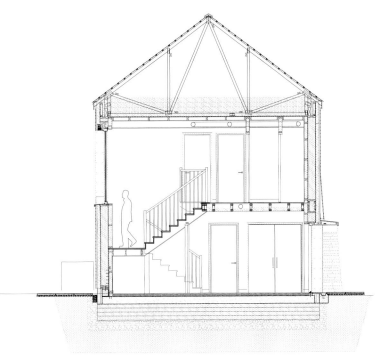

Left: Larch House from north.
Right: Section.

Top: Larch House from south with terrace and garden.
Bottom: View from street with small windows towards north.
Right: External window detail.

Iselisberg

Uesslingen, Switzerland
Architect: Honegger Architekt
Completion: 2011
Client: Confidential
Certificates and standards: Minergie-P Eco
Sustainable techniques: Warm air heating system with heat recovery
Photos: Pierre Honegger, Herdern

This Minergie-P-Eco certified house is located in an idyllic village, on the edge of the residential zone in Iselisberg Uesslingen. The new buildings within this residential zone have timber constructional elements and replace old farmhouses and service buildings. The modern architecture references the surroundings volumes, roof forms and materials. The two halves of this semi-detached family house are divided by a two-story storage space, which functions as a washing and hobby room on the upper level. The houses are heated exclusively by comfort ventilation and are equipped with photovoltaic panels, which allow a positive energy balance to be achieved.

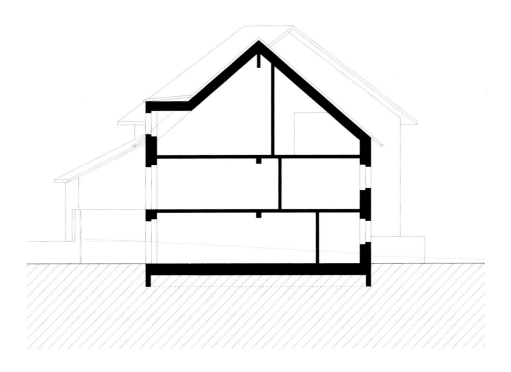

Left: Front view with terrace.
Right: Section.

153

Top: Dining area with kitchen and glass front.
Bottom: Living area with staircase.
Right: Exterior view from north.

The Cape Schanck House

Cape Schanck, Australia
Architect: Paul Morgan Architects
Completion: 2006
Client: Paul Morgan and Anna Pearce
Certificates and standards: Passive House certified
Sustainable techniques: Water tank stores rain water and cools temperature of living room
Photos: Peter Bennetts, Melbourne

This design was created using computer renderings and wind tunnel tests on a cardboard model and was then placed within an expanse of smooth native elements – wind forces, vegetal phototropism, diurnal sunlight movement, rain patterns. The form modeling produced an aerodynamic external skin and continuous internal skin. Wind turbulence at the entrance zone resulted in this section of the skin being different. In the living room, the ceiling swings down to an internal water tank. Water is harvested from the entire roof area and is stored in the tank during the summer. The tank cools the ambient air temperature of the living room in the warmer months, supplies rain water for toilets and gardening and structurally carries the roof load.

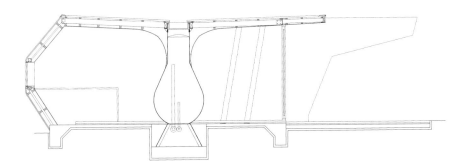

Left: Rear view from tree canopy.
Right: Section, with water tank.

Top: Cape Schanck view from street.
Bottom: Living room featuring bulb tank.
Right: Front bedroom.

Energy-Saving House in Frauenau

Frauenau, Germany
Architect: oberprillerarchitekten
Completion: 2008
Client: Thomas Killinger
Certificates and standards: Primary energy demand 14kWh(m^{2}a)
Sustainable techniques: Solar panels, passive solar energy use, concrete core activation, log boilers
Photos: Boris Storz, Munich

This house serves as a retirement home and office for a teacher and author. The program required that the house be low budget and largely energy self-sufficient, situated in the orchard of the client's parents' house. The concept design is rural in scale and proportion and has a translucent exterior façade, which references local glassmaking traditions. The double façade functions as communication space, mediating between inside and outside and functioning as an unheated air buffer. A minimalistic approach to technology and construction was accomplished by the use of intelligent planning and pure materials. The building's energy-architecture results in even less energy being used than required to fulfill Passive House standards.

Left: Exterior view from southeast with terrace and solar panels.
Right: Section.

Top: View from garden with terrace and glass front to the south.
Bottom: View from north.
Right: Detail of the façade cladding.

Green-Eco-House

Buxheim, Germany
Architect: Fabi architekten
Completion: 2008
Client: Confidential
Certificates and standards: KfW-Energiesparhaus 40
Sustainable techniques: Heat pump and ground collector, solar system, controlled ventilation with heat recovery, rainwater collection
Photos: Herbert Stolz, Regensburg

The context of the environment, together with the wishes and demands of the clients significantly influenced the design of this house. The house is sustainable, maintenance-free and energy-self-sufficient and the design ensures health and comfort in a technical and structural way. The house meets KfW 40 building standards and has a primary energy demand of 36kWh/(m²a). The future-oriented building technology boasts a heat pump with a geothermal heat collector, 12-square-meter solar thermal system for domestic water heating, photovoltaic system for electricity generation and uses graywater for toilet and garden irrigation. The result is a building that is environmentally friendly, energy-efficient and carbon neutral.

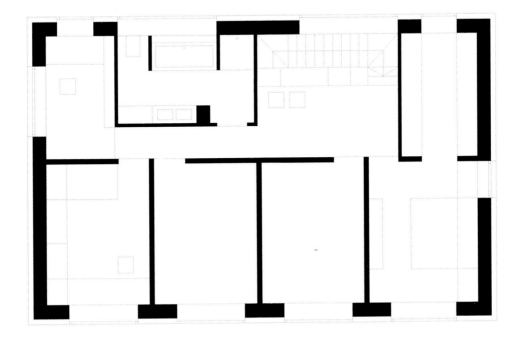

Left: Southern corner with glass front.
Right: First floor plan.

Top: Southeastern corner with terrace.
Bottom: Interior view with kitchen.
Right: Detail of eastern façade.

Maison Damico

Mesnil Saint Denis, France
Architect: Karawitz Architecture
Completion: 2010
Client: Benoit Damico
Certificates and standards: Passive House certified
Sustainable techniques: Ecological materials, extremely low-energy consumption, rain water storage tank
Photos: Mischa Witzmann

This Passive House is located to the north of the Chevreuse Valley, in the town of Mesnil Saint Denis. The valley acts as a green corridor between plateaus to the north and south. The house is designed around the principle "the cheapest energy is that which is not consumed" and requires no heating, due to the level of insulation and the use of bioclimatic principles. Power for heating water is supplied by solar panels. The exterior design is particularly coherent, built from solid wood panels, insulated with wood fiber and covered with larch cladding. The windows are triple-glazed, which helps to insulate the house. Collected rainwater is used for washing and gardening, significantly reducing the amount of wastewater.

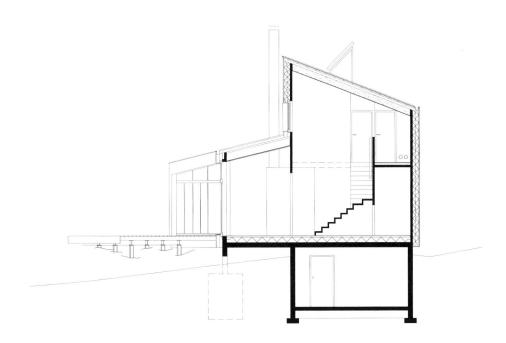

Left: Exterior view with entrance.
Right: Section.

Top: Side view.
Bottom: Exterior view with glass front.
Right: Detail of façade and trible-glazed window.

Schwalbenstrasse Passive House

Wetzikon, Switzerland
Architect: Honegger Architekt
Completion: 2006
Client: Stockwerkeigentumsgemeinschaft Schwalben
Certificates and standards: Minergie-P
Sustainable techniques: Warm air heating system with heat recovery
Photos: Pierre Honegger, Herdern

This Minergie-P certified family house is situated on the outskirts of the town of Wetzikon. The building has been constructed with wooden design elements and the façade with vertical timber formwork. The three separate units are connected by means of a glazed corridor. The bedrooms, with shower and bath, are located on the upper floor and a metal pergola with a timber grid stretches the entire length of the south façade. The three houses are heated exclusively by comfort ventilation and are equipped with photovoltaic panels; these achieve a positive energy-balance. The boundary walls are made of recycled building elements and water collected from the roof of the house is used for the swimming pond.

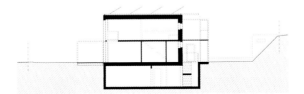

Left: Exterior view from northwest with entrance.
Right: Section.

Top: View from southwest with garden and terrace.
Bottom: Open bathroom on upper floor.
Right: Dining room with gallery and glass front.

Rimrock Ranch

Pioneertown, CA, USA
Architect: Lloyd Russell
Completion: 2008
Client: Confidential
Certificates and standards: California Title 24
Sustainable techniques: Passive cooling with thermal mass
Photos: Dave Harrison, San Diego

Rimrock Ranch is a vacation home with a flexible program that allows it to become either a two-unit rental or a permanent home. The shade structure combined with the insulated concrete slab on grade is a passive, low-tech solution that allows the house to engage rather than reject the desert climatology while employing an inexpensive strategy to achieve grandeur and intimate scale simultaneously. This scale shift allows the individual spaces to connect to larger spaces yet remain small making it easier and more cost-effective to build, maintain and condition. To date, the air conditioning, although provided, has yet to be turned on.

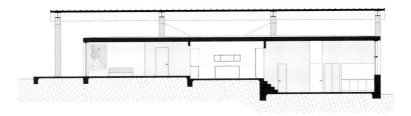

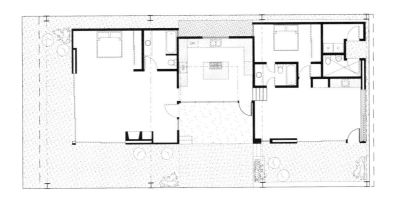

Left: View of patios and walkways.
Right: Ground floor plan and section.

Top: South view.
Bottom: Exterior view at dusk.
Right: Interior view of master bathroom.

Residence for a Briard

Culver City, CA, USA
Architect: Sander Architects
Completion: 2008
Client: Thomas Small and Joanna Brody
Certificates and standards: LEED Silver
Sustainable techniques: Passive heating/cooling, natural daylighting, recycled construction materials, super-insulated, graywater storage for landscape
Photos: Sharon Risedorph Photography, San Francisco

Residence for a Briard is one of the greenest houses in California. The structural frames, exterior walls and roof were all prefabricated off-site by warehouse manufacturers. These pieces were then simply bolted together. Once the shell was finished, all interior walls, systems and finishes were completed in a traditional manner. The client is a music critic who requested that string quartets could come and perform in the house. Consequently, Sander Architects provided a room surrounded by a suspended balcony. Passive heating and cooling techniques are used to reduce energy usage and the house is insulated with recycled blue-jean insulation. Natural daylight is also optimized throughout the house, reducing electrical energy usage.

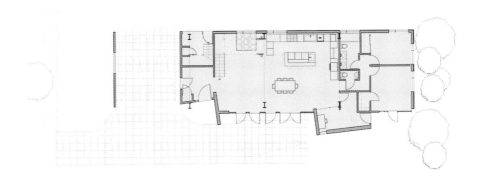

Left: Balcony from upper office overlooks yard.
Right: Ground floor.

Top: Exterior façade by twilight.
Bottom: Translucent panels at night.
Right: View of spiral stair to upper office.

House by the Lake

Zurich, Switzerland
Architect: m3 Architekten, Zurich
Completion: 2008
Client: Confidential
Certificates and standards: Minergie
Sustainable techniques: Geothermal heat pump, comfort ventilation, photovoltaic
Photos: Bruno Helbling, Zurich

The starting point of this project was the existing building. The task was to bring the restrictive requirements of the authorities in line with the wishes and demands of the client. A partial demolition and reconstruction was licensed, which led to the creation of a new building. The ground floor of the original building was demolished and rebuilt. With a wood-system construction the building receives a projecting upper floor. A façade of wooden slats was constructed, giving the house an open appearance. The ground floor consists of an open space with a weatherproof terrace. The house is Minergie certified and uses geothermal energy and comfort ventilation. Photovoltaic panels are also utilized to make optimal use of the sun's energy.

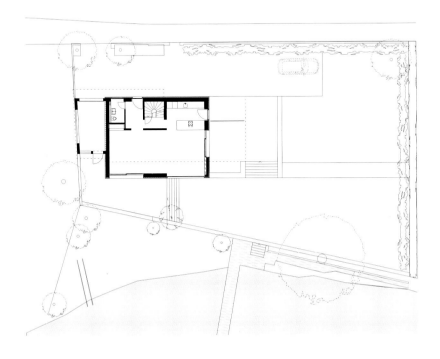

Left: Exterior view, with terrace and lake.
Right: Ground floor plan.

Top: Exterior view with garden.
Bottom: View from children's room.
Right: Cantilever shaded terrace with view to the lake.

Urban Reserve 22

Dallas, TX, USA
Architect: Vincent Snyder Architects
Completion: 2008
Client: Diane Cheatham, Urban Edge Developers
Certificates and standards: LEED Gold, Energy Star HERS 50
Sustainable techniques: Passive cooling, roof angle designed to accommodate future solar panels
Photos: Charles David Smith, Dallas

The client, who is a developer and contractor and has lived in this home at times, desired a contemporary residence to serve as a prototype demonstrative of the values of a 50-lot sustainable development in suburban Dallas. In addition, the design is for 'empty nesters' who enjoy entertaining and hosting; everything from small intimate dinners to large gatherings. Lastly, this is a zero-lot line development where all homes will be located directly on the north property line. The lots are narrow and must include a six-meter-wide yard on the south. No views are permitted to the north into adjacent lots. A highly protective roof envelope constructed of ventilated slate is shaped to control heat gain, gather cooling breezes and collect rainwater.

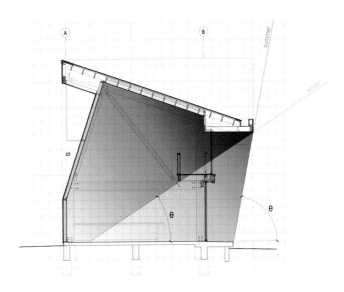

Left: Southern glazing to side yard.
Right: Section solar diagram.

Top: Northwest corner with access through bridges.
Bottom: Southern glazing to side yard.
Right: Entry with roof angle designed to accommodate future solar panels.

Orange Grove House

Melbourne, Australia
Architect: Fiona Winzar Architects
Completion: 2010
Client: Miriam Bereson and Adam Nissen
Certificates and standards: Australian 5 Star Energy Rating
Sustainable techniques: Insulation, passive heating/cooling, renewable timbers, water storage, solar hot water
Photos: Shania Shegedyn, Melbourne

The experience of living in this home is akin to living in a tree-house. Facing onto an adjacent park, the first floor living level features a double height space that provides spectacular views over the park's gum trees. In a positive move to densify inner city suburbs, this project involves a subdivision and a new residence. Although the new house has a small footprint, the three levels allow for a generous family home with room for a courtyard and vegetable garden. The north facing aspect and a five star energy rating ensures a sustainable future for its inhabitants and will provide a precedent for sustainable development in the city.

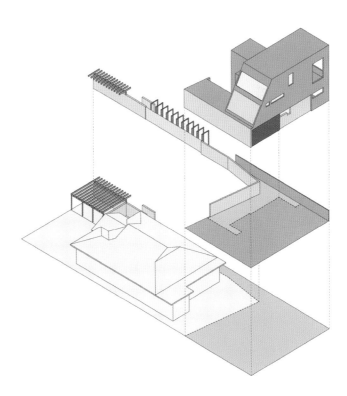

Left: The courtyard entry features twin rain water tanks.
Right: Three-dimensional graphic of subdivision, new boundary walls with entry path and new house.

Top: View to mezzanine over dining and kitchen beyond.
Bottom: Timber cladding blends with the environment and the living level is elevated to face onto trees.
Right: Materials blend with the rear laneway.

Passive House M

Haiterbach, Germany
Architect: m³ architekten, Stuttgart
Completion: 2010
Client: Confidential
Certificates and standards: Passive House certified
Sustainable techniques: Ventilation system with heat recovery, LEDs for illumination, solar collectors, rain water tank
Photos: Daniel Stauch, Stuttgart

This certified Passive House is located in the middle of the Black Forest in Germany. The building's north side is relatively closed, while the south side is fully glazed and adapts to the sloping terrain. All interior rooms are oriented in the direction of the valley, an orientation that offers privacy from adjacent properties. With its unobstructed views of the valley and peaceful location, the aesthetic nature of the building is emphasized by both its playfully and curving exterior and its interior technical functionality. In addition to the ventilation system with heat recovery, solar collectors on the roof support a domestic water heater and buffer. In line with the Passive House concept, the house is heated primarily through ventilation. For additional comfort, under floor heating has also been integrated.

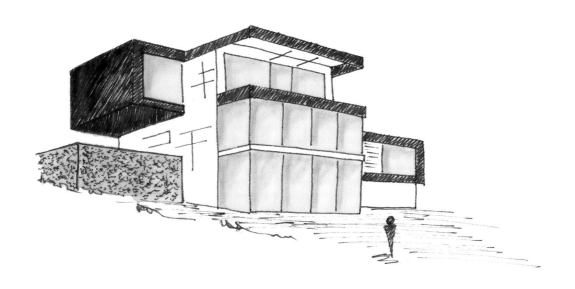

Left: Glazed south side adapted to sloping terrain.
Right: Sketch.

Top: House offers unobstructed views of the valley.
Bottom: Dynamically curving aesthetic black ribbon.
Right: Glazed south side optimizes views of valley.

Birds Island

Kuala Lumpur, Malaysia
Architect: Graft
Completion: to be determined
Client: YTL Green Home Competition
Certificates and standards: Zero Energy
Sustainable techniques: Lightweight bamboo frame covered in fabric reflects sunlight
Photos: Courtesy of the architects

Graft have applied an integrated strategy of developing a zero-energy house that seamlessly dovetails the economic and environmental advantages of environmentally friendly living, with the needs of a demanding and cosmopolitan clientel. The primary living space is concentrated inside cooled zones. A maximum amount of economical and energy efficient floor area is created and sheltered from the elements by a dynamic tensile structure. Extended living spaces are arranged separately from each other and bisected by landscaped areas with local vegetation. The surrounding tensile fabric flows through the interior, imbuing the spaces with sublime shading and view patterns.

Left: View from lake.
Right: Section.

Top: View by night.
Bottom: Bird's-eye view.
Right: Detail of the interior.

JustK

Tübingen, Germany
Architect: amunt - architekten martenson und nagel theissen
Completion: 2010
Client: Confidential
Certificates and standards: Passive House EnEv certified
Sustainable techniques: Ventilation system with heat recovery, geothermal heat exchanger
Photos: Brigida Gonzalez, Stuttgart

The tower-like cubature, distinctive shape and sloping roof and walls of this hillside house represent an unusual approach to passive construction. The spatial layout of this low-budget residential home, designed to accommodate six people, is sophisticated and exciting; it can also easily be divided into two independent residential units. A tight construction timeframe and the desire for sustainability made a wooden structure the inevitable choice, allowing optimum application of prefabrication technology. The choice of materials, including interior surfaces of treated, laminated wood, combed plaster base and the homogenous roof covering, all underscore the defining concept.

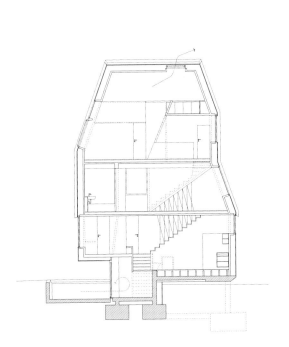
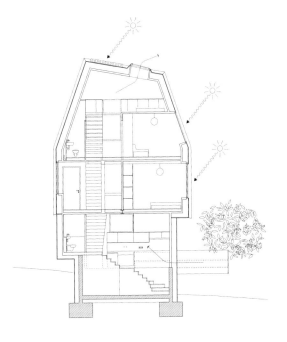

Left: View from northeast with direct access to the garden.
Right: Sections.

Top: Tree canopies from the neighboring garden visually enclose the living-room.
Bottom: The cantilevered balcony extends the kitchen-living room.
Right: The south-facing façade is largely glazed for maximum solar gain.

Plus Energy House in Kasel

Kasel, Germany
Architect: Architekten Stein Hemmes Wirtz
Completion: 2009
Client: Confidential
Certificates and standards: Plus Energy House, Passive House certified
Sustainable techniques: Natural building materials, green roof, photovoltaic system, isofloc insulation, CO_2 neutral building materials
Photos: Courtesy of the architects and Linda Blatzek

This Plus Energy house is located in the wine-growing community of Kasel, Ruwertal. The building is used as an office, but can be converted to a home if needed. According to the construction program, the house has been designed as a Passive House. The highly-efficient building design is supported by solar energy elements, allowing it to reach the Plus Energy standard. The design of the massive, elongated timber construction is modern and uses eco-friendly, local building materials, such as oak and slate. The same materials, in reduced form, have also been used in the interior.

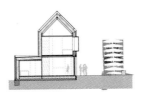

Left: Exterior view from north.
Right: Elevations and section.

Top: View from street.
Bottom: Interior detail of library/meeting room.
Right: Entrance and reception desk.

Bridge House

Ashbourne, Australia
Architect: Max Pritchard Architect
Completion: 2008
Client: Confidential
Sustainable techniques: Solar panels
Photos: Sam Noonan, Adelaide

Bridge House is designed to allow appreciation of the site without spoiling its beauty. Two steel trusses are anchored by four small concrete piers, poured each side of the creek. Spanning between the trusses is a concrete floor slab on steel decking with a layer of rigid insulation. Insulation on the underside of the slab, wall and roof combined with double glazed curtained windows aid the retention of heat. A small wood combustion heater provides additional heat when required, fuelled by timber grown sustainably on the site. Roof water is collected for use within the house. Wastewater is pumped 100 meters from the creek to avoid pollution and dispersed underground following treatment. Photovoltaic cells power the house.

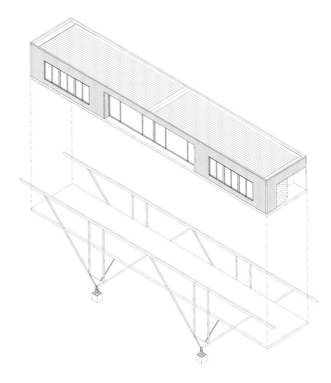

Left: Elevated building.
Right: Axonometry.

Top: View from living room to garden.
Bottom: Building spans across the river.
Right: Detail of the façade.

Zuber House

Pszczyna, Poland
Architect: Peter Kuczia
Completion: 2011
Client: Confidential
Certificates and standards: Low-energy house
Sustainable techniques: Solar panels, passive and active solar energy, high insulation standards, biomass heating, rain water reuse, recycled building elements
Photos: Lukasz Urbanski, Cracow

The design of this house was inspired by the place and its traditional architecture. The economical layout and compact shape of the building save resources, energy and money. The structure is divided into two blocks: one with a double pitch roof clad in fiber cement and another – used temporarily – with a flat roof and timber façade. The house utilizes passive and active solar components, green materials and technologies, including recycled materials, solar panels and high performance insulation systems. A green roof planted with drought-resistant plants cooperates in reducing heat transfer through the roof. The house was built on a very limited budget.

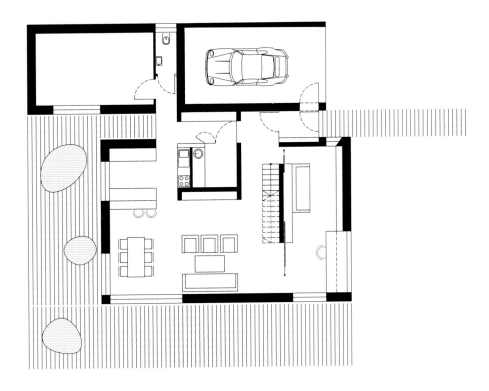

Left: Exterior view with terrace.
Right: Ground floor plan.

Top: Façade clad in fiber cement.
Bottom: Details of the fiber cement and timber façade.
Right: Passage between the two blocks.

House in Gerês

Gerês, Portugal
Architect: Graça Correia
Completion: 2006
Client: Confidential
Sustainable techniques: Local materials and man power used to build house, no trees were cut down during the construction process
Photos: Luis Ferreira Alves

This project involved the reconstruction and augmentation of a ruin into a weekend retreat. The chosen plot had extraordinary characteristics, situated near to the Cavado River and its tributary. The clients desired that the exceptional view should become an integral element of the house, while the architects aimed to create a large, spacious interior. The weightless intervention, enhanced by the overhanging part that shoots off the riverbank, maximizes the transparent appearance from the river, reducing land occupancy and avoiding all existing trees that provide shade on a hot summer day.

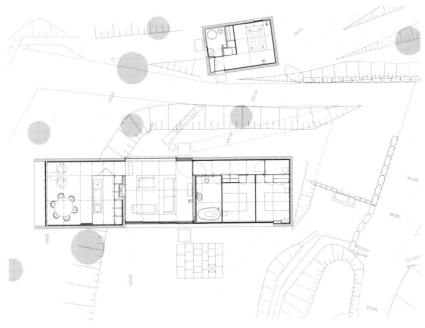

Left: The house rests like a stranded boat on the shore.
Right: Site plan, with ground floor plan.

Top: Large windows forge a link between the house and nature.
Bottom: View towards the river.
Right: The ruin neighboring the house is a constant presence.

Caterpillar House

Carmel, CA, USA
Architect: Feldman Architecture
Completion: 2010
Client: Confidential
Certificates and standards: LEED Platinum Custom Home, Energy Star, California Title 24
Sustainable techniques: Photovoltaic system, rammed earth walls, passive heating/cooling, insulation, rainwater harvesting system
Photos: Joe Fletcher

The Caterpillar House is the first LEED Platinum Custom Home of the Central Coast. The client came to the project with a love of modern ranch houses and a desire for an environmentally conscious response to the beautiful site. The construction and operation of the home minimize environmental degradation within the nature preserve. The gently curving, rammed earth walls act as a thermal mass, regulating temperatures from day to night. Capturing rainwater for irrigation, three tanks proudly sit close to the home. The glazing, natural ventilation and operable shading also act as a passive heating and cooling system. Integrated photovoltaic panels enable the house to produce enough energy to meet all of its requirements.

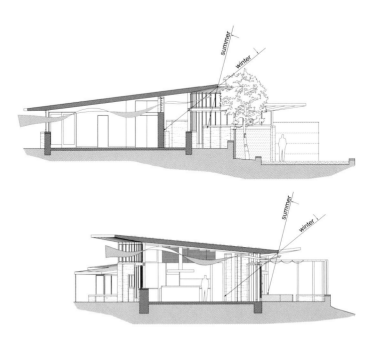

Left: Glazed façade and large roof.
Right: Sustainability section diagrams.

Top: Terrace overlooking the landscape.
Bottom: Storing 103,342 liters of rainwater for irrigation, three tanks sit close to the home.
Right: Walls built with earth excavated from the site.

Passive House Mini115

Imst, Austria
Architect: Mario Handle
Completion: 2010
Client: Confidential
Certificates and standards: Passive House certified
Sustainable techniques: Compact ventilation, small heat pump, air and water heating, domestic hot water storage, timber frame construction, cellulose insulation, petroleum-free materials
Photos: Mario Handle and Christian Klingler

With the right concept a Passive House can be absolutely affordable. The Mini 115 is the epitome of high efficiency on a small budget. Anything unnecessary has been omitted; the building envelope has been optimized and the distances minimized. Design challenges have been 'naturally' resolved where possible. By using natural materials and shading, each individual element of the design has a practical sense. The Passive House Mini115 is characterized by larch wood, the wooden panels are a simple yet elegant solution, offering shade and providing some privacy from the south. The Mini115 is part of a series of so-called 'Mini-Houses', whose motto is clarity and minimalism.

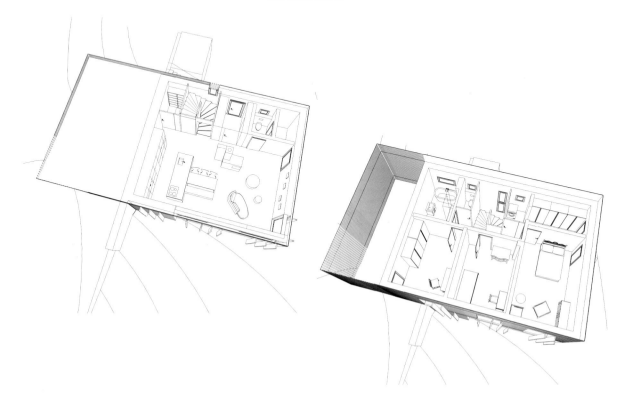

Left: Front view with mountains in the back.
Right: Ground and first floor plans.

Top: View of living room.
Bottom: Interior, living room.
Right: Wooden façade with glass front and terrace.

CO$_2$-Saver House

Lake Laka, Pszczyna, Poland
Architect: Peter Kuczia
Completion: 2009
Client: Confidential
Certificates and standards: Polish Passive House standard, Polish Green Building Council Best Sustainable Building without Certification, Best Silesian Architecture
Sustainable techniques: Passive and solar energy, heat recovery, thermal zoning, recycled aggregate, high insulation standards, airtight ventilation engineering
Photos: Tomek Pikula, Cracow (232, 234 a., 235), Peter Kuczia, Osnabrück (234 b.)

This simple sustainable house blends into its surroundings like a chameleon. Located near Lake Laka in Upper Silesia, the house has a timber façade of colored planks which reflect the tones of the adjacent landscape. The design of the house aimed, not only to integrate the building into the environment but also to ensure low construction costs. All details are simple but well thought-out. Costs were minimized by the application of traditional building techniques, the use of natural and local materials, like untreated larch and the use of recycled building elements. The built form was additionally designed to optimize the absorbance of solar energy.

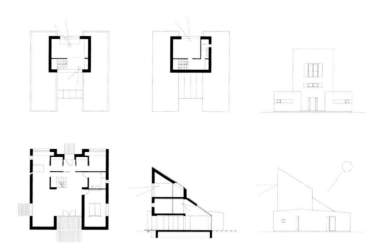

Left: Detail of the façade with view from southwest.
Right: Floor plans, sections and elevations.

Top: Exterior view from south.
Bottom: Interior view with winter garden.
Right: Detail of wood-clad higher part of the building.

Index

Architects

Places